10
TOP TIPS TOP TIPS

on **Placing Disabled Children**

Hedi Argent
with Robert Marsden

BAAF
ADOPTION
& FOSTERING

Published by
**British Association for Adoption & Fostering
(BAAF)**
Saffron House
6–10 Kirby Street
London EC1N 8TS
www.baaf.org.uk

Charity registration 275689 (England and Wales)
and SC039337 (Scotland)

British Library Cataloguing in Publication Data
A catalogue record for this book is available from the British Library

ISBN 978 1 910039 21 2

Project management by Miranda Davies, Publications Department, BAAF
Designed by Helen Joubert Designs
Typeset by Fravashi Aga
Printed in Great Britain by T J International Ltd

Trade distribution by Turnaround Publisher Services, Unit 3,
Olympia Trading Estate, Coburg Road, London N22 6TZ

BAAF is the leading UK-wide membership organisation for all those
concerned with adoption, fostering and child care issues.

Contents

Introduction   1

Tip 1: Know the child before learning about the disabling condition   4

Tip 2: Check your attitudes to disability   10

Tip 3: Respect the birth family and the child's need for continuity   15

Tip 4: Be aware of the resources available   21

Tip 5: Consider the choices   25

Tip 6: Think *because* of, not *in spite of*, disability   31

Tip 7: Find the right family   36

Tip 8: Prepare *this* family for *this* child   42

Tip 9: Prepare *this* child for *this* family   50

Tip 10: Devise a robust placement support plan   56

Ten more top tips from an adoptive family
Robert Marsden   66

Appendix   75

Bibliography   81

Useful organisations   88

This series

Ten Top Tips on Placing Children with Disabilities is the 13th title in BAAF's *Ten Top Tips* series. This series tackles some fundamental issues in the area of adoption and fostering with the aim of presenting them in a quick reference format. Previous titles are:

- *Ten Top Tips for Placing Children*, by Hedi Argent
- *Ten Top Tips for Managing Contact*, by Henrietta Bond
- *Ten Top Tips for Finding Families*, by Jennifer Cousins
- *Ten Top Tips for Placing Siblings*, by Hedi Argent
- *Ten Top Tips for Preparing Care Leavers*, by Henrietta Bond
- *Ten Top Tips for Making Introductions*, by Lindsey Dunbar
- *Ten Top Tips for Supporting Kinship Placements*, by Hedi Argent
- *Ten Top Tips for Supporting Adopters*, by Jeanne Kaniuk with Eileen Fursland
- *Ten Top Tips for Identifying Neglect*, by Pat Beesley
- *Ten Top Tips for Making Matches*, by Jennifer Cousins
- *Ten Top Tips for Supporting Education*, by Eileen Fursland with Kate Cairns and Chris Stanway
- *Ten Top Tips on Going to Court*, by Alexandra Conroy Harris

Details are available on www.baaf.org.uk.

Note about the authors

Hedi Argent is an independent family placement consultant, associate trainer for BAAF and PAC-UK and a freelance writer. She has worked for local authorities and was a founder member of Parents for Children, a voluntary adoption agency that pioneered the placement of older children, sibling groups and children with disabilities. Hedi is the author/editor of more than 20 books on adoption and fostering, including several for young children.

Robert Marsden trained as a social worker more years ago than he cares to remember and has spent most of his life working with children. His adoptive son has cerebral palsy and the author tells his story in *The Family Business* (BAAF, 2008). Readers might also be interested in seeing a short film about him made by his brother Tom. This can be found at: www.vimeo.com/84565880.

Acknowledgements

I am grateful to the children, their families and carers who have taught me all I know about disability. Their stories have been amalgamated and their names have been changed to preserve anonymity, but this book could not have been written without them.

I also want to thank Shaila Shah, Director of Publications, Miranda Davies and Jo Francis at BAAF for their unfailing support and patience, and Phillida Sawbridge for her helpful comments on the manuscript.

Introduction

> *First we're a family with two children. Then we're a family with two adopted children. Last of all we're an adoptive family with two disabled children. Remember that.*
>
> Adoptive parent

The aim of this book is modest; it will neither present a research and policy review of permanent care for disabled children who cannot remain with their birth families nor offer a guide through the labyrinth of health, education and social services for children with disabilities, which may, or may not, be available in this or that area. *The Good Practice Guide: Every child is special* (Cousins, 2006) and *Taking Extra Care* (Argent and Kerrane, 1997), both published by BAAF, do all that and more. This slim volume is more of a checklist to keep at hand for whenever a child with a disabling condition needs a new family. The ten top tips offer a starting point and signposts to further reading and helpful studies.

Until the mid-1970s, children with even the slightest disability were not considered to be candidates for adoption; in order to avoid any mistake, "unfit for adoption" was frequently stamped on the front of their file. Change came in the mid-70s inspired by pioneering work in the US (Sawbridge, 1975), influenced by the seminal British Study, *Children who Wait* (Rowe and Lambert, 1973), and encouraged by adoptive parents who spoke from experience. By 1976, a few specialist agencies were finding and supporting permanent new families for the most severely and multiply disabled children. But as often happens in social work, the pendulum is swinging again, and a high percentage of children who are lingering in care or on the Adoption Register have some degree of disability, and adoption is not routinely considered for children with more complex conditions.

Definitions of disability vary. The medical model is limited to chronic conditions that can be diagnosed and may, or may not, respond to treatment. The UK government's definition is taken from the Disability Discrimination Act 1995: 'A physical or mental impairment, which has substantial and long-term effect on the ability to carry out normal day-to-day activities'.

However, there is a "social model", which defines disability in terms of 'the combined effects of impairment and social oppression'; as one 14-year-old wheelchair user explained: 'it isn't my legs that make me handicapped, it's the places that don't have ramps for my wheelchair.' The last two definitions are echoed in the statement of the World Health Organisation, which describes disability as 'restriction or lack of ability to perform an activity in the manner or within the range considered to be normal'. This seems to be the most helpful way to view disability in regard to the children who need new families.

So why and when do children with disabilities need permanent foster care or should they, and can they, be adopted? Do we try hard enough to keep them in their own families? Can residential care ever be the placement of choice for disabled children and should we therefore assess and prepare residential facilities as thoroughly as we assess and prepare new parents? How should we recruit and support families for disabled children? Can we work directly with all children however seriously impaired? Should a disabled child be separated from a sibling group? How vital then are issues of ethnicity, religion and culture for children with disabilities? How do we deal with safeguarding issues and how do we work not only with birth parents who "can't manage", but also with parents who have harmed their disabled child and perhaps, worst-case scenario, have even caused the impairment?

These are some of the questions this brief book will address. But like all good answers, top tips should lead to more questions. Creative child placement work must always ask questions and not take "no" for an answer. If we ask enough questions, fewer children with disabilities will remain in care.

It is gratifying that attitudes towards disability seem to be becoming more positive as disabled people become more visible in public life and in the sports arena. There has recently been universal condemnation of "commissioning parents" who have rejected disabled babies born to surrogate mothers, and strong support for the surrogate mothers who have kept their disabled children.

The material in this book is divided into ten top tips with a bonus at the end. A parent who adopted a boy with cerebral palsy 13 years ago, adds his own ten top tips for social workers. He reminds us that no matter how hard we try to get it right, no one can foretell exactly how it will be when *this* child is placed with *this* family. That is perhaps even more true for disabled children than it is for all children.

Hedi Argent
October 2014

3

TIP 1

Know the child before learning about the disabling condition

> *Do you know who you are? You are a marvel. In all the world there is not another child exactly like you. In the millions of years that have passed, there has never been another child like you.*
>
> *From a Jewish prayer to welcome a new child into the community*

Every child is special and has special needs. Children with disabilities may be more special with more special needs. They are "children in need", and according to the Children Act 1989 (England and Wales) and the Children (Scotland) Act they should qualify for a whole range of services to meet their special needs. Even so, it has been found that it costs three times as much to bring up a child with disabilities than a child who is not disabled (Baldwin, 1985); there has not been a more recent study to contradict these figures. It is therefore not surprising that lone parents and families on a low income are most likely to have the hardest time to meet the special needs of their disabled children.

Unfortunately, some children with disabilities become "looked after" by local authorities because they need a degree of care that their parents cannot provide or cannot go on and on providing; it should never be the case that children come into care because enough help or the right help is unavailable. Others have to be removed from their homes and parents because they have been neglected or abused, often as a member of a sibling group. Relatively few are rejected or abandoned only because they are disabled.

Every child is a child first and a disabled child maybe

It is sometimes easy to overlook the child and concentrate on the disability. Most of us are not familiar with the details of disabling conditions and quite correctly set out to learn how this or that impairment may affect this or that child. But before we come to grips with the impairment, we need to know the child, just as we need to know all children before we find them a family.

Points to consider

- What were this child's antenatal, birth and postnatal experiences?
- What kinds of attachments have been made and broken?
- What losses and separations has the child endured?
- Who are the significant people in the child's life now?
- Has the developing brain been injured by emotional or physical trauma?
- How does the child deal with rage, shame, impulse and stress?
- Can the child show empathy and trust?

- Does the child see the world as a good or a bad place?

- How has this child developed emotionally and socially?

- Who does this child perceive to be her sisters and brothers?

- What is this child's role in the birth family?

- How far is the child's behaviour directly related to events?

- How does this child make other people feel?

These are questions we need to ask about any child we want to know. When the child is disabled, it may be harder to read the signals. Present and past carers, teachers and members of the child's birth family may all have something to contribute. And we then have to learn about the disability in relation to this particular child, for no two children will be affected in the same way by the same disabling condition.

Both of our adopted sons are on the autistic spectrum. They're as different as any two boys can be. We have to stop people treating them the same just because they both have the same disability.

Adoptive parent

Good observation, hearing and listening to people who have lived with the child, attention to detail and careful recording will lay the foundation for good reports. Paediatric, psychological, developmental and educational assessments will be required to give information, share opinions and offer advice to social workers and later to prospective carers regarding a specific child with a specific condition. It can be frustrating if social workers have to identify experts who may or may not have the time to respond. It is helpful if local authorities can establish a panel of professionals with an interest in disability who can be called upon to work together to present a rounded picture of the child's condition.

Don't be disabled by disability

- What are the causes, symptoms and prognosis of a specific disability?

- Is treatment available and desirable? For instance, what would be the advantages and disadvantages of heart surgery for a child with Down's syndrome?

- If the condition is not specific, should a diagnosis be pursued? For instance, "global developmental delay" may be impossible to define, but "learning difficulties" may have particular causes that require an educational assessment (see Bartram, 2013).

- Will the condition become more or less disabling as the child grows up? Is it a progressive disability like cystic fibrosis or is the impact finite as in Down's syndrome?

- Does the disability affect life expectancy?

- Will the child become an independent adult? Or what kind of support will the young person be likely to need in order to become independent?

- Is the disability genetic/hereditary and what are the implications for the particular child?

There are additional factors to be considered when a healthy but "at-risk" child is referred for adoption, insofar as the result of genetic testing might influence decisions made on behalf of the child. However, it should not be assumed that genetic testing will be required before a suitable placement can be achieved.

Turnpenny, 2014, p. 52

- Is the child related to other people with the same condition?

- Is specialist support available from organisations, professionals and peer groups? (see Appendix)

- Does the disability qualify the child for allowances and benefits? Many agencies have welfare rights officers who can point families in the right direction and help them to fill in forms.

- Does the child have special educational needs and how will they be met? (See new SEND [Special Educational Needs and Disability] Code of Practice, available at: www.gov.uk/government/publications/send-code-of-practice-0-to-25)

- Does the child have medical needs and how will they be met?

- What is the evidence from research about the child's disability? It can be rewarding to research a specific condition together with a prospective family.

- If the child has multiple disabilities and different professionals are involved, will there be a named lead person?

- *How does the child view/deal with her/his disability?*

> *I have Down's syndrome and I am adopted. My family, especially my mum, are bonkers but nice. I am really loved and I love them lots . . . I do so many interesting and exciting things. Down's syndrome and being adopted is OK by me.*
>
> *Boy, aged 14, quoted in Sturge-Moore, 2005, p. 6*

If we miss the opportunity to know the child, we will not be able to tell prospective carers who the child is. Misleading or inadequate information can lead to the child not being placed or to the placement disrupting. Distressed prospective adopters at disruption meetings frequently say that the child who came to live with them is not the child they were told about.

> *I think our social worker did his best but he didn't know Dillon any better than we did and we didn't know him at all.*
>
> *Prospective adoptive parent at disruption meeting*

There may often be confusion about what is due to the traumatic impact of a child's negative experiences and what is due to the impact of a disabling condition. Furthermore, many disabled children have multiple, related disorders. There are few certainties in getting to know a child, but an awareness of the complexity and observation of this particular child will combat unhelpful labels and categories.

TIP 2

Check your attitudes to disability

Check your own attitudes

- Do you truly believe that children with complex and severe disabilities can be adopted or do you think it is more realistic for them to be fostered?

- Do you believe that negative reactions to impairment can be more disabling than the impairment itself?

- If you believe that every child is unique, how can you avoid defining children by their disability?

- How much do you believe that ethnicity, religion and culture matter to children with disabilities?

- How far do you think you can work with every child, however disabled that child may be?

- Do you believe there is a family out there for every child, and that if we haven't found it, we haven't looked hard enough?

It seems to be true that the most challenging children, including children with disabilities, are successfully placed for adoption when their social workers are totally convinced and confident that this is the right plan and that it can be achieved; when it is plan A and there is no plan B. This does not mean that all disabled children who need care should be adopted; there will be children both disabled and not disabled for whom foster care will be the placement of choice, but it should not be the second best choice – children should not be fostered instead of adopted *because* they are disabled. In order to be convinced and confident that adopters can be found, it is necessary to be part of a convincing organisational structure with confident values and a robust support system.

> *I never thought of adoption when Tracy was allocated to me – I thought foster care because she was in a wheelchair. We didn't get much about adoption or disability on my course. This placement has been an eye opener to me because everyone is totally committed to getting disabled children adopted. That's what they do.*
>
> Student social worker

Popular images create social opinions and attitudes. Tiny Tim, in Charles Dickens's *Christmas Carol*, is not only very small but also wise, brave, exceptionally good and unlikely to grow up; he, like many disabled children presented in the media, elicits pity and a desire to rescue – not a good basis for adoption. The one-eyed Cyclops in *Ulysses*, Caliban in Shakespeare's *The Tempest* and Darth Vader in *Star Wars* display disability as a scary affliction, while adults with disabilities are widely featured to raise money for a raft of charities, thus leaving an impression of either dependence or undesirable "otherness". These negative images can seriously affect disabled children and lead to low self-esteem and identity confusion: 'Am I Ali who can't walk unaided or am I a wheelchair child?' (Ali, aged 12). If disabled children have to be separated from their parents and homes, their confusion and feelings of worthlessness will be even greater: 'They didn't want me because I'm handicapped' (Ali).

It is to be hoped that the growing interest in the Paralympics and the individual athletes who are not pathetic, scary or dependent, will influence public attitudes and encourage us all to become aware of the physical and social barriers we create to prevent people with impairments participating in day-to-day living.

There is no "kind" of child

It is not helpful to ask prospective adopters "what kind" of child they think they "can manage". It implies that children come in categories with problems that have, somehow, to be overcome. It is far better to stress the unique personality and attributes of every child and to allow families to respond to a specific child when they are ready. There is, after all, no real child between the ages of three and seven with ticked boxes of acceptable or unacceptable qualities. Adopters, when asked during preparation whether they would consider a child with "mild, moderate or severe disabilities", might say "no" to all three categories but surprise themselves when faced with an eight-year-old child who has spina bifida but also has courage, is curious and gentle and articulate and above all, needs a family to care for her.

> *We said we wanted to have a little girl under four to go with our two boys, and we said "no" to disability. Well, we didn't know any disabled children. But then we saw Zack in the newspaper and we fell for him before we realised he was sitting in a wheelchair. It was what he said about wanting a family to understand him that made us go the whole way. We're hoping to adopt a disabled girl later.*
>
> *Adopter of a boy with cerebral palsy*

If we label children as disabled rather than allowing them to be children first, we may not only be reducing their chance for a new family, but we may also be disabling them more than their impairment does.

Matching considerations

There is no reason to suppose that ethnicity, religion and culture are less significant for children with disabilities than for other children. In fact, it could be even more important for a disabled child, who perhaps cannot express her needs, to feel comfortable with new people who look similar to her birth family and enjoy a lifestyle and rituals that are familiar. It is hard enough to imagine how a child must feel if she has to leave her home and parents to go and live with strangers. It is harder still to imagine what that feels like if she has limited sight, hearing, understanding, language, mobility or any other disability. It is then sometimes tempting to concentrate on finding a family who can cope with the disability and to overlook other matching considerations.

Solly was a black African three-year-old boy diagnosed with severe global developmental delay. He was deaf and it was predicted that he would never learn to speak or to communicate. It was uncertain whether he would ever learn to walk. He lived with white foster carers and their three birth children.

The committed social worker in a pioneering agency was determined to find a permanent family for Solly. She was glad when a single black woman responded to publicity but did not fully appreciate the match until Solly was introduced to the prospective adopter. When she picked him up and held him, he gazed at her face and then slowly stroked her cheek and his own. There was no

> *question in the adopter's mind or in the social worker's: Solly had made the link.*

In the files of children with disabilities, it is sometimes recorded that direct work has not been undertaken because the child would not comprehend it or benefit from it. A photograph album may be the sum of their life story. But surely every child, beyond babyhood, who has to be introduced to a new family, has a right to know what is going to happen in some way they can understand? It is up to us to find out what that pathway is for each child. And if we cannot tread that path, there will be experts who can.

Kay Donley, the founder of Spaulding for Children, a pioneering adoption agency in the US, came to England in 1975 and inspired us to place older and disabled children for adoption. It was she who stated categorically that if we haven't found a family for a child, however old or disabled, we have not looked hard enough. And that rallying call is as relevant today as it was 40 years ago. Jennifer Cousins' review of children featured in *Be My Parent* during one quarter (Cousins, 2006) found that 40 per cent had some sort of "special need"; 20 per cent had significant impairments and 5 per cent had very serious impairments. That means that there are many children who will never have a new family unless we firmly believe that there is a family out there for every child and that we *can* go out and find it.

TIP 3

Respect the birth family and the child's need for continuity

When children with disabilities are taken into care, parents who already feel overwhelmed can easily be made to feel irrelevant. They may then limit or cut off contact in the mistaken belief that their child needs only people more expert than themselves. It is therefore particularly important to work as closely with the parents of disabled children as the situation allows. Families who cannot accept or cope with impairment may still have a contribution to make to their child's future care and they may be the experts in their child's specific disability. A receptive, sensitive approach to ethnicity, culture and religion will help to produce a well-balanced assessment. For instance, it is not helpful to assume that "all Asian families feel shame about disability" or that "all Jews prefer to look after their own".

> *The social worker was really good. She understood what we'd been through with Boris. We expected he'd have to go in a home but she persuaded us to let him go to a family that could look after him no matter what. They're still looking for the right family and they're kind of making us part of the plan.*
>
> Mother of five-year-old child with Down's syndrome and severe heart condition

Even if there are prescriptive court orders, parent may have unique knowledge about their child's disability. But it is hard for social workers, who have had the unenviable task of removing a neglected or abused child with disabilities from home, to treat the parents as equal partners in making a plan for care and continuity, or for parents to trust a worker who has taken their child away and who is not a disability specialist. In some such cases it may be helpful to appoint a new worker from a disability team who can re-focus on the child's and the family's special needs and strengths.

When birth parents have injured their children and caused the disability, any kind of contact becomes problematic, not only for the child and the parent but also for the new family. As one adoptive parent said, 'I want to be forgiving, I want them to know that Leah is surviving but then I see the other children play outside and I think, that could have been Leah but for you (quoted in Argent, 2003). However, children with disabilities, like all children who have to leave their parents, their families and their communities, have a right to expect that appropriate continuity will be preserved for them. It may be more difficult to find the right words or the right way, and children may have to be protected from further harm, but it is never good enough to presume that children are too disabled to be aware of loss of continuity or that contact has no significance. Even if a child cannot express their need or cannot show pleasure when they see a person who has been important to them, the loss of continuity is yet another social handicap that ought to be avoided. Joanne could not walk, talk or hear but her permanent foster carer was sure that visits from her birth father had a positive, calming effect on her: 'On some level she knows. It doesn't have to be on our level. She finds her own level in her own world.'

If continuity is interrupted for too long, birth parents may get stuck with their image of Jimmy as an immobile mute four-year old and be shocked to meet an adolescent with a deep voice and shambling gait who gives indiscriminate hugs to apparent strangers. Though adopters may be proud of Jimmy's progress, the birth parents may see only a painful reminder of his impairments. And Jimmy may have sustained an irretrievable loss.

It is not always easy for children to stay in touch with what may be a painful past. If they do not read or write, are unable to use the telephone, to walk or to travel unaided, then it is both more difficult and more necessary to help them. A child with a learning disability may never be able to make sense of their world if they lose their connections, or a child with a physical impairment might deduce that their disability destroys meaningful relationships.

> *My mum, she couldn't cope with the wheelchair, I expect she don't see me 'cause she's glad to see the back of it.*
>
> Girl with tetraplegia, aged seven

Sibling relationships

When a sibling group with one disabled child requires a permanent family placement, it is often the child with disabilities who is separated from sisters and brothers because she has "special needs". However, her greatest special need may be to retain her relationship with an older sister whom she can trust, and the older sister may suffer for the rest of her life if she "abandons" her disabled sibling. There may be defensible reasons for splitting sibling groups after a thorough assessment, but disability alone is not one of them. If more than one sibling is disabled, it may be wrongly presumed that no family can manage both, especially if the birth parents could not.

> *Margaret became a teacher for deaf children after her daughter was born deaf and later developed autism. Twenty years later she saw a feature about two deaf brothers, aged 10 and 12 who were also thought to be autistic: the local authority was looking for two two-parent families because both boys had to be closely supervised and it was thought that they didn't relate to each other. Margaret felt strongly that to separate the brothers would handicap them further and persuaded the agency that she could manage them together, given enough support. With a rota of paid and volunteer helpers she managed very well. She adopted both boys and organised their move together to fully supported independent housing when they were in their mid-20s. Margaret says, 'I have never doubted that it was right to keep them together. It would have been tragic if as well as losing their mother and their hearing they had lost each other; and I know whatever happens, they will not be alone.'*

Sometimes adopters have to convince professionals that continuity matters to a severely disabled child. Macaskill (2002, p.140) quotes an adoptive parent:

> *Julian missed his birth parents and wanted to see them. That was clear despite his disability. He was asking for them all the time in the only way he*

> *could. He was crying every day, 'Car-go-see-Nanny.'*
> *We had a car so he could not understand why we*
> *could not take him to see his Granny. He cried for*
> *over a year. It was a real bereavement.*

Julian's adopters finally persuaded the local authority to arrange contact. 'At the first meeting with his mother and grandmother, his facial expression lit up the room.' But it isn't always as straightforward as it seemed to be for Julian. Amber, aged seven, diagnosed with an unspecified global disability, has no words to describe her feelings. She sees her birth mother and siblings four times a year. When they come, she clings to them and ignores her single adopter on whom she is totally dependent; when they leave she is distressed. It is very upsetting for carers to witness this kind of behaviour and tempting to insist that their child should be shielded from more stress because she is already burdened by her disability. The question always has to be asked: whose needs are being met by maintaining continuity?

Some points to consider

- The safety of the child.

- The consequences of staying connected.

- How much can the child remember and for how long in relation to frequency of visits?

- What type of meeting venue is comfortable for the child?

- How much can the child benefit from other than face-to-face contact?

- If contact is not possible, what other means of preserving continuity are available? (for instance, videos or DVDs, social media, stories, photographs, visits to significant places).

- How far can the birth parents and permanent carers work together? (Even if the child is not capable of participating in arrangements, the good atmosphere generated by co-operating adults can have a beneficial effect.)

- The child's, the parents' and the carers' emotional resilience.

Birth families and carers usually need continuing support from professionals if continuity is to be maintained for disabled children. And social workers who support continuity also need good support and supervision from their managers.

> *A contact relationship between any birth parent and adoptive parent has the potential to be difficult but there are some additional complexities... when contact concerns a disabled child.*
>
> *Macaskill, in Argent, 2002, p. 144*

TIP 4

Be aware of the resources available

That first social worker, he went to a lot of trouble. He was like a special sort of person for Liam. He really knew him and he knew what was out there for him and that helped me too. But the second one – she just went through the motions and I knew more than she did.

Kinship carer at a peer group meeting

Legislation, regulations and guidance are in place for us to use in the best interests of disabled children and their families. According to the

Children Act 1989 (England and Wales) and the Children Scotland Act 1995, the disabled child's status, both in the community and in the "looked after" system, is that of "a child in need". Under the legislation, disabled children must be viewed as children first and their disability as a secondary, albeit significant, issue. Provision must be made to include:

- an assessment of need;

- access to all public services;

- services that minimise the effects of disability;

- a register of disabled children living within the boundaries of the local authority.

The guidance makes a distinction between disability and special educational needs: not all disabled children have special educational needs (though they may require aids to access the common curriculum) and not all children with a statement of special educational needs are disabled. Disabled children, of course, are also included in the regulatory framework for *all* children, so that the principles that must be applied are:

- The child's welfare is paramount.

- Children must be raised in their own families whenever possible.

- Children's wishes and feelings must be ascertained and taken into account.

- Local authorities have corporate responsibility for children living within their boundaries.

With the best of intentions, it is not possible to provide the service every disabled child and their family has a right to expect, unless the resources needed are available. Sometimes they exist but are not identified; more often they only become available when social workers and families can demonstrate a need and either create them or fight for them. The situation will vary in different regions and even in adjoining authorities. It is good to know what is offered where and what is not, in order to give families the kind of service described in the quotation at the head of this chapter.

Points to consider

- Does the agency have a clear and comprehensive policy about working with disabled children and their families?

- Is there at least one experienced disability worker or adviser attached to each team?

- Does the agency medical adviser refer families and social workers for guidance to relevant experts regarding specific disabilities?

- It is said to cost up to three times as much to bring up a child with disabilities as a non-disabled child. Are allowances generous enough to cover the extra costs incurred?

- What is the local situation regarding adaptations and mobility housing?

- Is there an opportunity for families to network and to have peer support from specialist organisations? 'The National Autistic Society was very helpful – they have a fantastic website and local self-help groups.' (Roberts, 2013, p. 63).

- Does the agency have a robust post-placement/adoption service tailored to special needs?

- Are there opportunities for professional training in disability issues?

- Is there an agreed route whereby families can get immediate attention and advice in an emergency?

- How is up-to-date information disseminated about disability rights and benefits, both locally and nationally?

- Which schools in the area offer the best education for which disabled children? Is there an education specialist in the adoption team?

- Are play/music/drama/therapies available locally, and are children with disabilities welcomed?

- Is there a disability specialist in the local CAMHS or are there other therapeutic services for disabled children and their families in the area?

- What are the play group/nursery opportunities for disabled young children?

- What are the local employment/leisure opportunities for disabled young people?

No one is anyone is going to have, nor will anyone be expected to have, all the answers to all the questions at their finger-tips, and they will not all be relevant to every child with disabilities. But it is important to be aware of what families might need to know and to be prepared to find the answers for them or with them.

> *It wasn't like she made herself out to be an expert in my son's rare condition, but she was on the case. We'd exchange and discuss odd bits of information we got hold of, and she was always willing to follow up. I think she learned as much about how to cope as I did.*
>
> Single adopter

TIP 5

Consider
the choices

The majority of children with disabilities who come to the attention of local authorities can continue to live in their own homes with one or both birth parents for most of the time in spite of the shock, grief and anger, the overwhelming exhaustion, the strain on relationships and the economic disadvantages often associated with having a disabled child. Birth families may then require a range of services in order to care for their child adequately, including regular short-term care with linked carers; sometimes the availability of the right respite family at the right time can prevent the escalation of problems necessitating permanent placement solutions, but as we have already seen, a large proportion of children coming into care have minor to severe disabilities.

Does the agency culture encourage social workers to explore the whole range of permanent placement options – including kinship care, residential care, special guardianship and foster care as well as adoption – for children with disabilities?

Family and friends care

For disabled children, as for all children, remaining within the wider family has to be the first choice decreed by law and common sense. Relatives and close friends have the advantage of sharing the family history (probably also the ethnicity, religion and culture) and of having an investment in keeping the child in the family. The details of kinship care arrangements will differ according to the legislation in Scotland, Northern Ireland, England and Wales, but the principles are essentially the same throughout the UK. All potential kinship carers should be informed of the choices they can make, of the regulations that may apply and of the support that would, or at least should, be available. Informal family arrangements, private fostering, local authority fostering and Special Guardianship Orders are the options. (See also *10 Top Tips: Supporting kinship placements*.)

> *Both my grandchildren were born with a disability because of my daughter's drink problem. I watched her struggle with them but she couldn't cope. The council said would I look after them, and I said yes but I didn't want them to be in care, I didn't want to foster, just to be their gran. But then I couldn't rely on my daughter and I needed a regular income, so I did become a foster carer at the end.*

An aunt looking after her nephews found fostering less rewarding:

> *We did need the regular pay, and we were worried about them turning up under the influence and taking the boys away, so we went for fostering, but what we didn't know was all the paperwork and the reviews in our house and having to keep a diary and all that.*

All kinship care pathways should leave the door open to accommodate changes in the family and the increasing needs of disabled children as they and their carers get older and may require added services and emotional support. What may have worked well enough as an informal private arrangement when the child was an infant could become a challenging placement when a physically mature adolescent is totally dependent on his carers.

Adoption

Adoption is still the only way to secure legal permanence for children who cannot remain with their birth families. It provides a substitute family not only during childhood but for life, which disabled children are even more likely than other children to need. Children with disabilities began to be successfully placed for adoption in the mid-70s by pioneering agencies refuting the accusations that second-class children were being matched with second-class families. It is true to say that unusual families were found for unusual children; horizons were widened but never lowered.

It has been shown that children, who in the early 70s would have remained in residential care, in hospitals or in residential schools can be placed with families who not only want them, but also grow to love them and enable their development and fulfilment beyond the expectations of social workers in the past.

Wedge and Thoburn, 1986, p. 78

If we believe that every child, however disabled, is adoptable, we also have to ask, as we do for non-disabled children, whether adoption is the best option for every disabled child who needs a new family. The government is enthusiastic about adoption in England and targets have been set for local authorities, which are measured on score cards, in order to speed up the process. But the score cards do not make allowances for the time it may take to find a family for a severely disabled child or how long it can take to prepare that family and the disabled child to make the transition to permanence. Decisions should always be made on an assessment of the child's needs, not influenced by a preference for already approved adopters or by competitive scores.

Permanent foster care

An arrangement that ends when the child is 18 (or even at 21 in special circumstances) is not as permanent as many children with disabilities are likely to need, especially if they have not maintained strong links with their birth families or are not able to make the transition to independence. However, if connections are nurtured, long-term fostering can be a way of sharing the care and may continue on a life-long informal basis for the benefit of the young person and both families.

Some families who are totally committed to a child may choose to foster rather than adopt because they do not want, or don't see the need to, take the child away from the parents; others, often already experienced foster families, fear that they will not get the support they will need if they adopt. Many foster carers who take disabled children with some apprehension apply to adopt years later, thus skewing the timescales on the adoption score cards but bringing lasting security to the young person.

> *We said we'd have a go – never had anything to do with Down's before – except we did have neighbours once with a grown son like that – but she was like ours from the start. She stayed when the others came and went. She's that close to us and loving, we could never have let her go. And she's going to need us for ever. So in the end we adopted her to make sure.*
>
> Foster carer/adopter of infant, now young person, with Down's syndrome

Special Guardianship Orders (SGOs)

An SGO, introduced in England and Wales in the Adoption and Children Act 2002, may be useful for disabled children because it takes them out of the care system and gives carers a measure of parental responsibility, legal rights and the possibility of local authority support without severing the legal connection to the birth parents. An SGO may enhance the stability and security of a kinship or stranger fostering placement, but like formal foster care, it terminates when the young person is 18, and is therefore not a real alternative to adoption. Also it is difficult for carers with an SGO to obtain an allowance commensurate with the expenses of caring for a child with special needs.

Residential care

It can be that parents want residential care because they think that, as they can't, only specialists can look after their disabled child, and it may indeed be the only way to provide expert care for a child with complex severe disabilities. At best, if carefully matched to the child's needs and if staff are as thoroughly prepared for a particular child as permanent carers would be, residential care could be the placement of choice. At worst, children with disabilities are placed in unsuitable residential homes because nothing else is available and no one is complaining or asking the right questions.

Sacha (now aged 11) was introduced to us gradually. She'd been with foster carers who'd done their best since she was a baby, but they couldn't cope when she got too heavy to lift. They knew how to communicate with her and they showed us. She's been living with us for four years now. We've got all the equipment she needs and we can offer her lots of learning and leisure opportunities. This is her home now but her foster carers are still her family.

Head of small residential home

Creative alternatives

It is important to keep an open mind when considering the permanent placement options for disabled children. As noted, long-term fostering arrangements can endure beyond childhood, and 'a creative continuum between adoption and fostering may reduce the barrier to permanence for some disabled children' (Cousins, 2005, p. 39). And only a small proportion of disabled children who come to the attention of children's services will require permanent new families. Many will need regular or occasional short breaks with linked, well-prepared and supported respite carers. A very few will flourish in special units with professional supervision. In one London borough, the housing department allocated a four-bedroom apartment for the Director of Children's Services to hold in trust for three disabled teenagers so that a permanent foster family could move in to look after them. The young people had lived together in a children's home for 12 years and would not be parted; the creative solution was that if they could not move to a family, then a family would have to move in with them.

However long or short, temporary or permanent, conventional or innovative family care for disabled children needs to be, nothing can be achieved unless the right families are recruited. And the right families are out there, waiting, like the disabled children, for the right publicity to lead to a match.

TIP 6

Think *because* of, not *in spite of*, disability

The question, 'Can this disabled child be placed with a family?' should not be asked; it should be re-phrased to pose a different question: 'After a careful assessment of this child's needs, is family placement the right option?' If it is, then is there perhaps something a little odd about the families who come forward and deliberately choose to take on the total responsibility for children with disabilities? Who are they? What are their motives? Birth parents of disabled children, who have become overwhelmed by the struggle of looking after them, may be suspicious of people who don't see the task as a burden; professionals are often dubious about the stamina of families and their ability to do what they say they want to do – especially in the case of a prospective single parent. Or if, like Sheila and Ben, they have a large mixture of adopted, fostered and birth children already. Is it likely they can take another child, especially one with profound disabilities?

When the last of Sheila and Ben's three adult children left home, they decided that there was nothing they liked doing more than being active parents. They heard of a baby with a fatal heart condition who needed to be nurtured until he died. They fostered the baby while he had a series of operations. He sustained brain damage but he survived and was adopted by Sheila and Ben.

Next came an 11-year-old girl who had severe learning disabilities as a consequence of physical abuse. She was followed by a boy with spina bifida and epilepsy. And so it went on. When the family was re-housed to give them more space, they adopted more children with disabilities. When Ben was made redundant, he became a full-time father.

Quoted in Argent, 1998, pp. 40–42

Some people start on the journey to adoption by applying for a healthy baby and then stretch to meet a greater need.

Alma and Shaun married in their 40s and were not surprised when they did not produce their own child. They were keen to have a family and applied to adopt an ordinary baby. When they saw the profile of a two-year-old with Down's syndrome, they began to think that she was the child they might have had, and that she needed them as much as they needed her. They adopted Sami and she became their cherished only child. Her disability was never denied, but they delighted in her progress. Sami learned to speak fluently, to read and to write

> *well enough to sort out the TV programmes she loved to watch.*

Most often people choose to parent a disabled child because they have personal experience of disability: they may have a disabled child already; they may have been brought up with a disabled sibling; they may work with disabled people professionally or as volunteers or know someone else who does. People sometimes describe themselves as being "into disability".

> *Cassie worked in a residential home with children on the severe end of the autistic spectrum. She left work to adopt one of them because she felt it was better to parent one than to work with many. She became a single mother and adopted two more children with other disabilities in due course.*

One group of potential carers is made up of people who are themselves disabled. This does not mean that they have any special right to care for someone else's disabled child, but it may mean that they are able to offer a unique role model, insight and expertise.

> *Sue was born with a syndrome that stunted her growth and made her infertile. Her husband, John, was partially sighted. They felt that their experience of being labelled and marginalised had prepared them for bringing up children with disabilities. They adopted a baby damaged by rubella before birth and later a girl with achondroplasia (dwarfism). Both children flourished with their disabled parents and grew up to value themselves as young people with disabilities.*

Many people find the inner strength and inspiration to offer something extra through their religion. Single people can often give the one-to-one attention disabled children require without neglecting anyone else. Divorced or remarried people may have become wiser in the process. Members of minority groups may have gathered the strength to go the extra mile for a disabled child. On the whole, what unusual people who successfully parent children with disabilities have in common is a proven record of overcoming problems, openness, flexibility, the desire to communicate and the ability to fight for rights. However, it would be as foolish to advocate that all unusual people make good parents as it would be to discriminate against them. Because a family who are Jehovah's Witnesses have adopted three blind children successfully, doubtlessly guided by their faith, it doesn't mean that other Jehovah's Witnesses will make equally good parents. If some single adopters can give more undivided attention to disabled children, it doesn't mean that they all can. If a lesbian couple are the right family for one child, it doesn't mean that all lesbians and gay people should be given preference. Just as there are some common positive qualities, there are some common danger signals:

- *Rigid attitudes* – disability is not predictable; diagnosis and treatment may change as the child develops.

- *Too ready anger towards authority* – carers of disabled children may have to fight on their behalf, but they also have to be able to work closely with a host of specialist agencies and organisations.

- *Fear of being seen as "different"* – it is not a good thing to pretend that the disability factor or the adoption factor is unimportant or to expect people "not to notice".

- *Social isolation* – people who exclude themselves or others are not likely to help disabled children to integrate.

- *Pursuing a quest* – adopting a disabled child can become a crusade, with the emphasis on moral/social/political rhetoric rather than the child's best interests and needs.

The last point may seem like a contradiction of the title of this chapter, but it merely highlights the fine line between wanting the child for who she is and wanting the child in order to make a statement. A single parent, who adopted a severely disabled child with a limited life expectancy, taught me an invaluable lesson. I asked her, 'How can I tell whether someone can really be the right family for a child with profound disabilities?' Her answer was simple: 'It depends on whether they have found the beauty spot.' I had never heard her say this and I was taken aback. 'What is Joe's beauty spot?' I asked her. She seemed surprised that I didn't know. 'Why, his silence,' she said. Joe could not speak but communicated in a variety of other ways with his adoptive mother.

TIP 7

Find the right family

Every child deserves an individual recruitment campaign to find them a family. Just as there is no "kind of" child, so there is also no "kind of" family. There is a danger that untargeted recruitment strategies will result in a group of approved adopters and a group of children with specific needs, who are no match for each other. The new two-stage assessment process in England offers an ideal opportunity for avoiding this unhelpful state of affairs by allowing prospective adopters to respond to publicity after the initial safeguards and references have been completed; the second part of the assessment can then centre on the needs of a particular child. But families can only respond if they are exposed to publicity about the children who need them. A profile in a photolisting magazine may catch someone's attention but it is usually not enough; it is only the beginning.

There were all these children in the magazine and I think we were just bowled over by so many. Then we saw an article in the local paper about one of the little boys we'd noticed, and that really spoke to us and we enquired about him and well, here we are with Mo. We'd never thought about a child with disabilities, but it was what it said in the article that got us thinking.

Adopter of boy with Noonan's syndrome

Writing profiles

Even if profiles are only the beginning, it is important to take them seriously and to make the most of them. Conveying the unique essence of a child is only possible if we know the child. There is a risk that disabled children are stereotyped as being brave, especially sweet and rewarding. But surely – and even more so if they have a troubled past – they are also as moody, selfish, demanding and confused as all children. And if we look through profiles it is amazing how many "hard-to-place" children are happy, full of energy, affectionate, curious and "a joy to look after". It would be reasonable for prospective adopters to wonder why these children are still waiting. It may be difficult to write a good profile without jargon like "meeting milestones", "needing firm boundaries" and "having good attachments" but we should try. Profiles are not a sales pitch; children should not be exposed to vying with each other for attention.

When a child is disabled, we have to find the right balance between describing the real child and the child's disability – the balance between engaging the reader and telling it as it is.

A voluntary agency, having three male infants with Down's syndrome to place, put their profiles in a newsletter. Two of the babies were more or less similarly described as cuddly and alert, learning to smile, making good progress, eating and sleeping well and needing lots of love and stimulation to reach their full potential. The third was described as having been born prematurely, having a bit of a lopsided face, a hole in the heart that would have to be mended, hair that stands up like a brush and floppy limbs that would strengthen with exercise. The third baby received more enquiries than the other two put together and was placed first. When the adopters were asked why they chose him, they said it was because he sounded more real and needed a family most.

Argent, 2006, p.6

Recruitment campaigns

The profiles in the newsletter sent to people already known to the agency, referred to above, were only part of the campaign to get these three children placed. An area was identified where there were particularly good services for children with disabilities, including an active branch of the Down's Syndrome Association. Leaflets were distributed in local libraries, health centres and places of worship. A reporter from the local newspaper was approached and agreed to write an article about the campaign that included two other young children with disabilities. The culmination was an open meeting held in the local town hall and attended by 32 people. All five children were placed as a result: two were placed very quickly with families already approved by the agency; the other three families took longer to prepare, but there were added spin-offs. Children with disabilities who had not been featured in the campaign were eventually placed as a direct result of the interest aroused.

Adoption Activity days

It is not always possible to describe the complex attributes of any child, let alone a child with added special needs.

> *Myra was honestly and fully described in a published profile. She was unable to walk unaided and had only restricted speech. When she was introduced to an approved couple, they said, 'You, didn't say she was so withdrawn.' The couple didn't go on to adopt Myra. Later she was briefly introduced to a single carer who said, after meeting her, 'You didn't say she struggled when you try to help her.'*

One way of sharing information with prospective adopters is to let children speak for themselves – with or without the use of language! Two families can have entirely different reactions to the same child and perceive entirely different problems stemming from the same disability. It is common practice now to show videos before families commit themselves, but it is trickier to arrange face-to-face meetings. It is not acceptable to have children "looked over" and "blind viewings" incline towards a cloak-and-dagger approach. It is possible, however, to organise an outing for a group of children and to prepare a group of families to join the children in a day of activities. BAAF has developed a party model to introduce a random group of older children to a random group of approved adopters, resulting in many successful matches for participating agencies.

> *At first we didn't like the idea. We thought the children would feel embarrassed. But they didn't. They enjoyed themselves and so did we. Meeting Ali like that made all the difference. We may never have taken to him just from seeing his photo.*
>
> *Adopter linked with child after a BAAF Adoption Activity Day*

A different Activity Day model is perhaps more appropriate for children with disabilities; only families who have expressed an interest in one of a particular group of children featured in a publicity campaign, are invited to meet them. Families need not all be approved adopters, but they will at least have completed stage one of the assessment process. Activities can involve nothing more than playing in a soft environment, sharing meals, going for a walk and keeping tired children occupied. Such an Activity Day offers prospective adopters a down-to-earth opportunity to experience the real child and it can be a potential treat for the children. Only children who will enjoy the event, and won't find it disturbing, should be invited. The hard work comes in the follow-up – Activity Days are not a substitute for thorough preparation of linked children and families. The good news is that all the disabled children who have been included in this kind of event have been permanently placed, and the outcomes have resulted in high job satisfaction for the workers.

More targeted publicity

There are other ways to engage the attention of people who may become permanent carers of disabled children. Talks in churches, libraries or community centres can attract people who have never thought about disability. Local radio stations and newspapers may be interested in a story. Publicity aimed at organisations dealing with disability can attract people who have never thought about adoption. Letters to the editor of a specialist newsletter may raise awareness in general or produce a family for a featured child. A brother and sister, injured by their urban birth family, had a dream of living in the country. Only one family responded to a letter, written by the children's social worker to the editor of a farmer's journal – but it turned out to be the right family. A wide response to publicity is not necessarily better than a limited one. If a great many people become interested in one child, it may even be that the information was misleading.

An agency was flooded with enquiries about Joanna, an extremely pretty five-year-old child. The feature in a magazine fudged the fact that Joanna was on the autistic spectrum and had difficulty in sustaining relationships.

It is helpful if family placement teams can cultivate links with magazines that may be interested in being involved in recruitment campaigns for one child or a group of children. Magazines are a great source because they usually lie around waiting rooms long past their sell-by date.

If every child who needs a new family deserves an individual recruitment campaign, social workers must be given the time, support and supervision to create it. However departments are organised, the worker who knows the child and the adoption team have to get together to devise publicity, write a profile and produce material for features wherever they can be suitably placed. The important words here are "publicity" and "features", never "advertisements". There is nothing wrong with the true meaning of the word but it has become corrupted by marketing techniques and suggests that we are somehow trading in children. Birth parents are often horrified by talk of advertisements but may be more amenable to discuss featuring their child in publicity that has been individually and sensitively tailored to reflect their needs. What is more, most publicity, unlike advertisements, comes free.

This all sounds like a lot of extra work. It is not extra but essential if we really want to place children with disabilities, and if we firmly believe that if we haven't found the right family for a child, we haven't looked hard enough in the right places.

TIP 8

Prepare *this* family for *this* child

The 2014 Children and Adoption Act (England and Wales) stipulates that the assessment of potential adopters must be in two stages: Stage 1 for giving and recording information, for offering some basic training and to take up full references in order to assess the applicants' general suitability to adopt; Stage 2 for assessing the family's competence and capacity to nurture someone else's child. This second part will include an exploration of the applicants' flexibility, empathy, resilience, stability and sense of self; also their ability to overcome adversity, to co-operate and to manage "difference", conflict and dependence – all essential qualities for families contemplating the total and permanent care of a child with disabilities, whether through adoption or permanent fostering. These regulations offer a new opportunity to find the right match that is particularly relevant to disability.

There is no reason why prospective permanent carers, who have completed Stage 1 of the process and are therefore acknowledged as a safe pair of hands, should not be given the chance to "find their child" before they proceed to Stage 2. The home study can then concentrate on the needs and attributes of a specific child in relation to the carers' essential qualities, and offer the family an opportunity to decide for themselves if they think they can parent that child.

Access to the photolisting services of BAAF and Adoption UK (print and online), consortium newsletters, recruitment campaigns featuring specific children and photo sheets of all the agency's children waiting enables prospective carers to make that first amazing link with a child that "jumps out of the page" as one adopter has described it. This kind of "adopter-led" link may or may not result in a final "match", but it will certainly focus the minds of the family and social workers on a real rather than an abstract situation when it comes to the home study: How compatible are this family and this child? What can be done to prepare the family for this placement? And if *this* child for *this* family turns out not to be the right match after all, no harm will have been done: the child will not have been let down, which may happen during introductions if the child remains virtually unknown to the prospective carers; the family may or may not then be approved in the usual way, and if they are, they can go on to find another child.

> *When we adopted our son, we went through all that approval before we were shown profiles of several children that they thought were right for us and we felt really bad turning them all down. But we just knew we weren't right for them. Then when we thought we'd, like, failed, we saw this picture of Nicky and we just knew he was the one.*
>
> *Nicky's adoptive parent*

It would have been more helpful to Nicky's new family if they had been able to measure themselves against Nicky's needs during the second part of their assessment and been prepared by their social worker to meet them. If a child is disabled, it is even more important to have as many details and facts as soon as possible because not only are no two children alike, but the same disability does not affect two children in the same way.

What do prospective permanent families have a right to expect?

In Stage1:

- Information – about adoption and fostering, the agency practice, the assessment process, the children waiting for families including those with a range of disabilities.

- Access to information in books and online about specific disabling conditions. (BAAF publishes a series of short books called *Parenting Matters* that describe various disabilities and how adoptive and foster families have managed them.)

- Support to complete the initial application form – this can be achieved by the allocation of a "buddy" to save social work time. Buddies who are caring for a child with disabilities may help to widen applicants' horizons.

- Basic training, in groups, about attachment, trauma, loss, continuity, the kinds of children needing adoption and sibling relationships.

A helpful exercise to keep disability on the agenda is to hand out slips of paper to group members with a brief description of a behaviour or stage of development, for instance: is dry at night, says first words, has tantrums, can wash and dress unaided, can tell right from wrong, can remember directions, can be relied on, etc. Ask everyone to put their slips into boxes labelled: age 0–2, age 2–4, age 4–5, age 6–8, and so on. Read out the contents of each box in turn and discuss in relation to traumatised/ disabled children.)

- Discussion about purpose of references and medical reports, suitability of referees and outcomes leading to completion of Stage 1.

The in-between stage:

There are many well-established ways of enabling prospective permanent carers to gather information about the children who are waiting locally, in a consortium or wider afield. Some agencies have made innovative attempts to engage applicants to pursue the more "hard-to-place" children. Activity Days have already been described and will fit well into the in-between stage. At an "Opening Minds" evening in one local authority, prospective carers who have completed Stage 1 are invited to watch DVDs, speak to the children's social workers, and meet the agency medical adviser, who will discuss the implications of diagnosed impairments as well as the uncertainties of developmental delay. People really have opened their minds as a result, and disabled children have been securely placed with families who were encouraged to make the link.

Let us suppose that the applicants have seen a wide range of publicity and have responded to a child with a diagnosed disability.

Stage 2:

- If the focus throughout the home study is on how *this* child would fit into this family and whether that family could meet the child's needs, then all the usual and necessary exploration of the prospective carers' competence and capacities can be related to testing their compatibility.

- All the information available about the child should be shared with the prospective family. There is nothing that people who may be entrusted with the total care of any child should not know; if the child is disabled, there is even more they should know. The more curious people are about a child, the more likely they are to bond with him or her; a thirst for information is the beginning of bonding. A Child Appreciation Day towards the end of this stage is an invaluable investment of everyone's time. It is best to make it an informal day, without a Chair or minutes, where previous and present carers, teachers, social workers, therapists and doctors can freely speak about the child and exchange views and anecdotes.

The aim is to present a multi-faceted picture because no two people see a child in exactly the same way. And how does the child make them feel?

> *At a Child Appreciation Day a foster carer, who was used to looking after several children short term, described a six-year-old girl with global developmental delay as being 'a right little pickle; she keeps me on the go, you never know what she's getting into, it's like dealing with a naughty toddler. But at the end of the day, when she gives you that smile of hers and wants a cuddle, she's the one that makes me feel good.'*

- A family meeting during the home study can be a good way for prospective carers to engage their older children and the wider family in their plans. If family members feel included, they are more likely to support the decision to bring a disabled child into the family; if they have experience of disability, their contribution and getting them on board in time can contribute to making a placement work.

- One of the best ways of helping families to consider the practicalities of caring for a specific child with disabilities is to do an exercise with a 24-hour clock. Using a large round diagram divided into 24 segments, they are asked to fill in everything they do in a normal day and night, including sleep. They are then asked to add in what the child they have in mind might be doing: Are their activities compatible? Is there enough space in the day for the child? How could they make more space? And how do they feel about broken nights?

- How do families think they are regarded by others, and how do they imagine they will be seen with the disabled child they have in mind? How will they deal with ignorant, offensive comments and how will any birth children they have be affected?

> *A parent took her ten-year-old birth daughter and five-year-old adopted son with cerebral palsy to the supermarket. Her daughter became deeply upset when she overheard a woman say: 'they ought to let them die when they're born like that'.*

- What are the rules, values, systems in this household that this disabled child will, or will not, be able to comprehend, appreciate or adhere to? Perhaps applicants can write down their family rules in three columns: rules that are unimportant in the first column, rules that matter but may be broken without consequences in the second, and finally those rules that may not be broken. People frequently insist that there are no rules in their family, but when they remember that children may not help themselves to sweets but are expected to help themselves to fruit, that the lavatory is not to be flushed at night, or that shoes have to be taken off indoors, the three columns begin to fill up. If the prospective family is a couple, do they both agree on the categories? Can they contemplate living with a child who may not be able to understand what is `expected of them?

> *Seven-year-old Ranjit, who had Down's syndrome, also had a craving for milk. Nothing his new family said could stop him from finishing up all the milk in the fridge whenever he had the urge. The adopters didn't want to put a lock on the fridge because that would have been against their principles, but they did want to have milk for a cup of tea. Finally they found a solution. They put a pint of milk in the fridge every day and kept a small jug of milk out of reach on a high stone shelf in the larder. Luckily they lived in the country where cool larders were still in operation!*

- Families usually prepare information to introduce themselves to the child. When the child is disabled, something more than verbal and visual means may have to be devised. A piece of music, their recorded voices, a particular perfume, a piece of cloth or an object that the child can learn to associate with the new family – sent by the family just for her – may mean more than words and photos in a book.

- If applicants are aiming to meet the needs of a particular disabled child, they will be better placed to devise introductions that take account of the child's disability. How much information can the child understand and retain? How can the child become familiar with people, places, smells, sounds? How well does the child travel? What will make the child feel relaxed, safe, interested, anxious, confused, angry or overtired? A discussion about introductions, even before getting to the stage of introductions, can be a useful tool to assess the suitability of a match.

> *Prospective adopters of a blind child, aged four, sent her a necklace, a small bottle of scent and a recording of nursery rhymes together with a description of their family on tape. When they met, the mother was wearing an identical necklace and using the same scent. Every time the child visited their home during introductions the same recording of nursery rhymes was playing in the background.*

- If disabled children require a lot of equipment, it may be a good idea to enable prospective carers to "practise" during this second stage. Some aids are complicated to use and getting to grips with them can distract from the child herself. An adoptive parent of a girl who is tetraplegic was perplexed by the electric wheelchair and nervous about using it. She said to her social worker: 'When you do this next time, place the wheelchair first.'

- Exploring together with the prospective carers the probable support needs of child and family can become an illuminating part of the assessment and result in a realistic, comprehensive post-placement plan.

An approach that gives applicants a chance to make the link with real children puts families, not social workers, in the driving seat. It avoids families being ruled out, or ruling themselves out, in the early stages for a disabled child they might never have considered in theory but could be the right parents for in practice. We have to trust that no one will deliberately set out to have a child whose needs they cannot meet; the second stage of the assessment can give potential carers the opportunity to assess, together with their social worker, whether what they *want* to do is what they *can* do.

TIP 9

Prepare *this* child for *this* family

In *Taking Extra Care* (Argent and Kerrane, 1997, p.75), Ailee Kerrane wrote:

> *The more I am involved in working with, thinking and writing about practice involving disabled children, the less difference I can see from the work with non-disabled children. The message is: don't be paralysed by the child's disabilities. Use the same basic principles as you would to work with any child. We might have to seek help about communication skills, find out about different impairments and strive for equality of services for disabled children, but we do not require a completely different set of skills.*

> *The key word is "adapt". Let us adapt our knowledge of child care to the world of the disabled child.*

It is not possible or desirable to approach work with disabled children as though they were a homogenous group. An eight-year-old with a physical impairment could be intellectually advanced for his age, while a child of ten with severe learning difficulties may have the understanding of a three-year-old and a child with minor disabilities could be seriously affected by emotional problems. But no child who has to move to a new family is too disabled to be informed about what is going to happen in some way that she or he can understand, however limited or unconventional that understanding may be.

> *Wise parents do not take their toddler on an aeroplane without first explaining that they will fly in the air, but they will surely not go on to explain aerodynamics, although a little information about seatbelts, length of the trip, funny feelings in the ears, and food available on the way would not come amiss. When the child is older, the information can be more detailed and technical, but the purpose will be the same: to allay anxiety about the unknown and to make the child feel confident about the journey. Children who have to separate from their home and parents are truly going on a journey, and if they are disabled, it is an extra factor to take into account when designing each child's package of travel information.*
>
> *Argent, 1997, p.66*

Nearly all children want to know at some level, although they may not be able to ask directly or even indirectly, the answers to at least some of these questions about their journey:

- What exactly is my disability and what does that mean for me?

- Why do I need another family? Is it because I am disabled?

- What is adoption, foster care, residential care, respite care?

- Are there other children like me?

- Will I still see my mum, dad, gran, auntie, brother, dog and anyone else I want to see?

- Why must I have my photo taken?

- How and where do you find families?

The most important part of preparation for permanence follows when a family has been identified. It is not possible for any child to visualise and anticipate an abstract " forever family" but when disabled children are matched with a family, they will want to know about them as all children do, and they may have particular concerns:

- Do they know I can't walk? Are they strong enough to lift me?

- Will my wheelchair go in?

- Have you told them I need help to go to the toilet, to get dressed, to wash?

- Will they understand me when I speak funny? Do they know sign language? Can they read braille? Will they understand that I can't always hear what people say?

- Will they get cross when things are broken because I'm clumsy?

- Will they cope when I have a fit?

- Will they know how to give me my injections?

- Will they stay with me when I have to be in hospital?

- Will they be patient when I don't understand?

And the ultimate question:

- *What happens if they can't manage?*

It can be very helpful for children to write notes or send messages to prospective linked adopters with all their questions, and for the adopters to reply. It offers reassurance to the child and gives the adopters yet another way to get to know about their child-to-be.

Life story work

With increasing demands to meet targets, to complete forms and to comply with new legislation, working with children who are not clamouring for it, can easily be cut short, delegated to the least experienced worker or left to the good intentions of foster carers, who, it is true, probably know the child best, but are not usually qualified to do focused direct work on their own.

Life story work is not a one-off event completed in a hurry when a permanent placement is imminent. It is the open-ended record of a child's life and a preparation for the transition to permanence. It does not have to be neat, chronological, or put together in an album with photographs. The contents of a box can tell a tale; DVDs, a roll of wallpaper, an inter-active picture book or website may appeal to the child. Anything that is meaningful for him or her can be included: a bus ticket or sweet wrapper may trigger a memory; a scribbled drawing may be significant. However it is done, it should reflect the child's continuing story so that the past is connected to the present and enables the child to contemplate the future.

Before Janine, aged four, who was blind and had severe learning disabilities, was introduced to her new family, her social worker guided her to fill a memory box with objects that had a meaning for her: wool from the foster carer's cardigan, a sea shell from a favourite outing, an audio tape of The Beatles, a piece of cloth sprinkled with her birth mother's perfume. Then they slowly added objects related to the prospective adopters: a tape with their voices and their dog barking, a handkerchief with a new scent, an acorn from their garden –

> *something new was added each time until introductions began and then the adopters helped Janine to choose an object every time they met.*

Even if a child seems to be too disabled to participate, he may respond to the attention of direct work, and the result may hold an indefinable meaning for him.

> *Five-year-old Damon, who had multiple disabilities and was apparently unable to communicate, would not be parted from his life story book. He tore all other books but not this one. Although he could certainly not comprehend his story, he somehow knew that it was his. He turned the pages carefully and laughed at the pictures.*

Involving the child

Before beginning to work with a disabled child it is essential to know how questions about the disability have previously been answered by parents and carers. Work can only progress if it starts from where the child is and it may have to progress very slowly at the child's pace. However, the process itself can be rewarding if children feel they are the protagonists rather than objects of concern. Even the most disabled children can be involved in some way in recording their story and in creating publicity to find a family: they can help to make posters (a handprint and footprint can be fun), stuff leaflets with their profiles into envelopes, and work the printer or photocopier to duplicate a newsletter. Working alongside the child offers the best opportunities for exploring their story and their understanding of it.

Lew, aged eight, had serious learning difficulties. His social worker could not engage him in any work to prepare him for the transition to permanent care. Only after several sessions "helping in the office" did the worker realise that Lew was stuck in searching for his mother, who had died when he was three. No one had ever explained her disappearance to him and he had no concept of "death" or of his own disability. Only after he was taken to see his mother's grave could he begin to concentrate on the present and look to the future.

This chapter must end as it began, by stressing that there is no dividing line between working with disabled and non-disabled children. All direct work has to be designed to meet individual needs and to match individual capacities; disability is one of many factors that will influence how an individual child can best be prepared for a specific family and how the child and family will need to be supported once a placement has been made..

TIP 10

Devise a robust placement support plan

> *One of the major barriers to placing disabled children for adoption is a potential family's fear that they will be left to battle with insuperable difficulties by themselves.*
>
> *Cousins, 2006, p. 47*

All children with disabilities have a right to specialist services and disabled children who are adopted or fostered of course retain that right. All adopted or fostered children and their families also have a right to be assessed for another set of support services. Both disability and permanent substitute family placement remain life-long factors. Should family placement workers know about the many aspects of living with disability? Should workers from a disability team know all about adoption issues? Should the responsibility for adopted and fostered children be transferred to an adult service when they reach the age of 18 or should children's services continue to support the placement until the young person achieves some degree of independence? Would it be possible, perhaps, for placement support teams and disability teams to work out a joint support package with and for each family?

Whatever the policy of the agency, families need clear messages about who will do what and who is qualified to do it. Families should never be left to disentangle the procedures and practices of various departments or left to "fall between two stools".

The adoption team expect us to slot into all the local disability services to get support, but then they send us back to the adoption people if we ask for help. And local disability groups don't really want us. It's like some of the other parents are saying 'you're not one of us, you've chosen to do this, we didn't have any choice'.

Adopter of child with Down's syndrome

Disabled children and their new families need services, but it is sometimes easy to confound them with well-meaning, indiscriminate support. Support is as good as it feels to the recipient; it can be that what we think is helpful is not perceived as being so; what is seen as supportive by one family can seem intrusive to another. What do families regard as support and what as supervision? We have to be very clear and careful about which we are offering.

> *Adam loves his bath. He likes to lie in it for a long time. I can lift him in and out quite easily but the occupational therapist wanted him to have a bath lift. But Adam wouldn't use it. They said I should try harder to get him used to it but he hated it and I asked them to take it away. Unless a mother is completely off the wall, she knows what her child needs and doesn't need. Like an electric wheelchair: someone once suggested Adam should have one, but what did they think he was going to do with it?*
>
> *Adopter quoted in Argent, 1998, pp. 12–13*

When a child has multiple disabilities, families can become inundated by well-meaning professionals who do not liaise with one another. One single adopter reported that she had a physiotherapist, an occupational therapist, her social worker, a welfare rights officer, a health visitor and play therapist visiting in the same week. It is helpful if a support worker can convene a meeting with the family and all the professionals involved with a child once a year to review the service they are offering and to make an integrated support plan for the next 12 months. Families may prefer to have meetings with professionals in their own homes or they may not.

Education

- Education can make or break a placement. The right special school or specialist department in mainstream can be of immense support to child and family, but no available school in the right area, or the wrong school, can put a placement at risk. New regulations (for England) regarding the educational needs of disabled children came into force in September 2014. They give parents more control over the support offered to their child including the possibility of direct personal funding. A single multi-disciplinary Health, Education and Care Plan is to replace the Statement of Special Educational Needs. Families will need help to negotiate the new system, which is intended to minimise the adversarial nature of the process.

Points to consider when making a support plan

- Some children want to have someone to talk to who is outside their two family circles, but others definitely do not. However, working with children should not stop when they are permanently placed. The emphasis on practicalities related to disability can sometimes lead to an avoidance of unresolved themes of loss and separation.

- One family may be well satisfied with relying on support as and when they need it, but others may need more regular contact with their post-placement worker. As one adopter put it: 'I know when she's coming, so I can save it all up and then I let it spill out and that kind of recharges my batteries.'

- Families may appreciate meeting with other parents who have disabled children, or they may feel that they have more in common with other adopters and foster carers.

The other parents with children with Down's syndrome treated us like we were either saints or mad for adopting Rafi. I suppose they had no choice and they complain a lot, which made us feel we couldn't keep on about how pleased we are with Rafi's progress. But the adopters' group understand, even if their children are not disabled.

Adoptive father

- What may seem like plenty of money to one person may not be enough for another. No one takes on the total care of a disabled child for profit, but families do have different requirements and aspirations, which should be respected. For instance, horse riding can be expensive, but it may fit into the family system and be a boon for some disabled children. Holidays abroad to include a child with disabilities may increase the cost more than a family can afford. As we know that it costs more to raise a child with disabilities, it would be unreasonable to approve families to do a job and then prevent them from doing it well for lack of funds. However, too much emphasis on financial support may be obscuring deeper reasons for concern.

- It is essential for families who are bringing up a disabled child to have up-to-date information about new disability legislation, rights and benefits, fostering and adoption regulations and research or advances in treatment regarding their child's disability. Busy families may not be aware of changes that could affect them and might welcome a newsletter with relevant information.

- Permanent carers of disabled children may wish for, and expect to have, short breaks at short notice, or they may prefer to plan their breaks a year ahead. It should be possible to provide what best meets their particular needs. Forms of support, like a home help, childminding one evening a week or an "adoption/foster care buddy" may be welcome. It can be hard to find a babysitter for even a small child with severe epilepsy. Something as mundane as smart disposable nappies or an incontinence service can make a difficult placement run smoothly.

- Families with disabled children too often have to fight for aids and adaptations, appliances, attendance and mobility allowances, suitable housing and transport. Some families are better at fighting than others, but a little help from their support worker will rarely come amiss, especially as all of this usually entails an awful lot of form-filling; people who make good parents are not necessarily as good at dealing with forms.

- One family may take complicated negotiations with medical experts in its stride, while another will need not only advice but also someone to support them and to interpret professional opinions.

We had all these students and doctors standing around asking questions, half of them we couldn't answer. They talked right over Matt as though he was a disability and not a child. We got so flustered in the end we couldn't really understand what they said about him.

Adoptive parent of child with multiple disabilities

- If families predictably need therapy or other specialised treatment for their child, they should not have to wait at a crisis point while experts are identified and funding is arranged. The route to treatment and source of funding has to be part of the support plan.

- Some permanent carers will welcome the opportunity to manage and maintain contact arrangements with birth families, but many will want to have social work support and guidance (see also Tip 2). In no case should disability be made a reason for discontinuity.

- If more than one agency is involved, it is vital to spell out who is responsible for what. It can be disconcerting for families to become aware that one agency doesn't know, or approve of, what the other agency is doing. "Splitting" between agencies can only lead to general mistrust with negative repercussions on the placement.

- Having a support worker from their own ethnic group may be significant for some families but not for others. *Cultural competence will be important for all.*

Training opportunities

Foster carers have a statutory obligation to continue learning; adopters do not. But this does not mean that they do not want, or should not have, further training opportunities offered to them. Sexual development, special education, alternative treatments, transition to independence, behavioural difficulties and welfare rights are the topics most carers with disabled children want to learn more about. It is not always necessary to hire guest speakers. There is often enough expertise among adopters and foster carers and it makes for a good day out if families can learn from each other and perhaps bring lunch to share.

> *An adoptive father who was a reflexologist showed how gently massaging feet is non-threatening for withdrawn defensive children, who fear physical contact and how it begins to build trust. This father also demonstrated, very movingly, how giving real attention is not at all the same as listening to a child with half an ear while peeling the potatoes. All the people who attended this workshop, including the adoption workers, took away new ideas to put into practice.*
>
> *Quoted in Argent, 2003, p. 186*

Many families will not be able to come to a training event unless their disabled children can come too. It is therefore essential to provide reliable and enjoyable care for the children, preferably in an adjoining room.

Practice issues

Support for permanent placements is enshrined in legislation, regulations, national standards and guidance. Fostering agreements and adoption support plans are intended to cover present and future needs and provision. Although the requirement for an assessment of adoption support needs is clear, the duty to provide is less specific. Families must know what will actually be offered and by whom: health, education, housing and possibly other relevant services also bear responsibilities for disabled children. An Adoption Support Services Advisor (ASSA) should be appointed by every agency to promote and maintain support agreements at a strategic level across departments and organisations. Although not prescribed, good practice would suggest that a foster care services manager has a similar role.

Support plans should never be tacked on as an extra at the end of the placement process. Discussion of what kind of support might be needed, expected and available is an integral part of assessment and preparation and should also inform permanency panel recommendations.

There are families who have the commitment, the energy and the vision to give life-long care to children with disabilities who have to be separated from their birth parents. There are disabled children who have enough courage and resilience to entrust themselves to new families. We must not expect the resulting placements to be better than the support we give to them. And we not only have to devise a support plan to match needs, we also have to implement it. Social workers come and go, departments are re-organised, legislation changes, but the support plan has to be sustained, reviewed and delivered if challenging placements for disabled children are to survive and flourish.

A final checklist

- *Services and experts*: Are they working together in the interests of the disabled child and family? Does the family have direct access to a named key worker? It is not helpful if anxious carers have to go through reception and a duty team before they can get the help they need.

- *Information*: Is the family kept up to date as planned? The same information may have to be given more than once at different stages.

> *It has helped having as much information as possible about parental substance misuse, FAS (Foetal Alcohol Syndrome), HIV and hepatitis. It has helped to talk to the doctor running the developmental clinic for children of drug abusing mothers.*
>
> Hartley, 2012, p. 93

- *Benefits and allowances*: Is the family claiming all entitlements? The welfare system is complicated and repeated changes in disability benefits can be confusing. Explanatory leaflets are helpful and there is up-to-date information on the internet, but an expert in the field who can guide families to make the right applications is usually very welcome.

- *Short breaks*: Are they available when and where the family needs them? In other words, are the arrangements family led and are links between permanent carers and short-break families nurtured?

- *Life stages*: Going to school and leaving school, significant separations, moves to independence – is support sufficiently responsive to the impact of change on a disabled child?

> *Our own social worker is exceptional. Being referred to the local child development centre within the first month, and referred a couple of years later to a psychologist who was experienced in adoption and attachment as well as autistic spectrum disorder, has been key for us as a family.*
>
> Hartley, 2012, p. 93

- *Contact and continuity*: Are arrangements working and are they regularly reviewed? If there is no contact with the birth family, how is continuity maintained?

- *Aids and adaptations*: Does the family have all necessary equipment as the child's needs change and possibly increase? Could an occupational therapist best advise a family what is available to suit their particular needs?

- *Education*: Has the combined health, education and care statement been completed according to the new legislation? Is it up to date and do carers/adopters agree with the recommendations?

- *Health*: Do families have satisfactory access to relevant treatments, assessments and therapies? If the child has a genetic disorder is continuing genetic counselling available?

A final word

> *When we took on the two boys we expected it to be hard going and it was. Looking back, we couldn't have got through it without our support worker. He was there for us and he never made us feel we weren't coping because we asked for help; it was like we were right to ask.*
>
> *Adopter of two brothers with severe learning difficulties*

Ten more top tips from an adoptive family

Robert Marsden

William came to stay with us when he was nearly four. Until then he had been in care almost continuously since birth, but had spent three years in the same foster care placement. The adoption was finalised about a year after he joined us. He is now 17. We first saw his profile in BAAF's *Be My Parent* newspaper. He was described as having cerebral palsy, having to use a walker, and needing daily physiotherapy from his carers; he had been born ten weeks prematurely and this was thought to be linked to his birth mother's lifestyle. Over the years his physical disability has become more profound. He cannot walk or sit unaided now and uses an electric wheelchair. He also has a visual impairment. He is more physically disabled than we thought he would be. But he has very good speech, an amazing memory for people and events, a brilliant sense of humour and a determined and winning personality. He is doing reasonably well at school and everybody loves him. He is our son, just as our three older birth children are, and they see him as every inch their brother. I think we were the only family who were seriously interested in adopting William. It is hard work caring for him – probably harder now in a physical sense than at any time in the past – because he is big, dependent, and a willful teenager, but we hope we have given him lots of love and a sense of security that he might not otherwise have had.

Tip 1

Be ambitious for disabled children

Like all children, disabled children will do best with new families if they are placed as young as possible. Some disabled children may have had a particularly traumatic start in life; they may have spent long periods in hospital after birth; they may have become disabled as a result of abuse or neglect. Our son spent his first three months in hospital without reliable consistent attachment figures. Children can establish attachments after such trauma, but the sooner they are placed with a family for life the more likely it is that they will be able to form secure attachments. Do not let children "drift" in care. Disabled children will be harder to find families for than other children, so you need to work especially hard to complete assessments and legal processes quickly.

Ambition for the child should not stop once a new family has been found. As a general rule the family should be *empowered* to care for the child; the more responsibility carers take on for the child's life, the more likely it is that they will be ambitious for them to meet their potential. Unfortunately there are battles to be fought in the world of disability to make sure children get the best services possible, the best education possible, the best chance of being all they can be. Disabled children experience more barriers in life than other children, and those caring for them have to have both an assertive and conciliatory approach in trying to overcome those barriers. For example, we had long negotiations with the local Cubs leader to see how William could be included; a lot of organisations claim to welcome children with disabilities, but in practice are totally unprepared to meet their needs.

There does need to be a word of caution, however, when talking about ambition: we need to watch that we do not expect children to be something they cannot be. When our son first came to live with us, we were told he would probably be able to walk with a walking aid. And for a short time he *did* walk with some support. But as he grew, his cerebral palsy had a greater impact. Despite all our efforts with physiotherapy he has become less mobile and generally more dependent. We had to help him adjust to this and change our own hopes and ambitions accordingly.

Tip 2

Remember that each child is unique

The needs of one disabled child will be quite different from the needs of another with a similar disability. They will have had different life experiences, will have different temperaments, will like different things, and so on. If you are trying to find a family for a child, you need to get to know them and their personality so you can describe them as a person, whether you are being cross-examined about their needs in court, describing them to a potential family or arguing for resources. If you know the child well and can talk about them with real commitment, you will maximise the chances of someone being able to see themselves caring for them.

Children with disabilities have particular vulnerabilities. They may not be able to articulate their needs,wishes and feelings in the same way as other children. You may have to learn new ways to communicate with non-verbal children. They are vulnerable because they are often very isolated and you have to work hard to ensure they are safe. You have a big responsibility to advocate on their behalf.

Tip 3

Share as much information as possible with prospective carers

Prior to making a decision about adopting William, we pored over his files, met with paediatricians and neurologists who knew him, spoke at length to his social worker who had known him and his birth family since he was born (a great advantage), met his foster carers and saw videos.

The more information prospective carers have, the better; you need to help them get into the role of parents for the child. Since we adopted William, Adoption Activity Days have been developed and these offer greater opportunities for would-be adopters to judge for themselves whether they could be the right family for a disabled child. It is important to stress to families that the future course of the child's disability is not predictable. We did not appreciate that William would end up as disabled as he has. As it happens, we love him very much and have adjusted our lives as he has become more disabled. The assurance of ongoing support to parents is very important. An adoption support or care plan that embraces the uncertainties of the future can be reassuring to families. Make sure you are going to stick to it, and adapt it as necessary throughout the child's childhood.

Tip 4

The emotional needs of disabled children are just the same as those of children who do not have disabilities

Without a doubt the most challenging aspects of William's care in the first few years were his grief at leaving his foster carers, his difficulty in making attachments, his rejection of us, his confused sense of identity, and the questions he kept asking about his birth family. Managing his physical disability was certainly challenging: initially it would take an hour and a half to feed him and then he would throw it all up again, but this challenge was nothing compared to the emotional impact on us of his challenging behaviours. Our love for him and his love for us did not come instantly. As with so many children with attachment difficulties it took time to develop. But it did come!

Children with disabilities may need particular help in managing their emotions, and sometimes their life stories can be painful for them to process. There can be difficult questions to answer about the causes of their disability, particularly if this is related to abuse or parental lifestyle, and why they are not living with their birth family. It is important to have a story ready for the child that is truthful, but geared to the child's level of understanding, and to tell it as sensitively and as easily as possible. We try to be matter of fact in our approach with William and we never judge his birth parents.

Tip 5

You should not assume that some children are unadoptable

Having a disabled child can fit in with the circumstances of some families; there are families with an amazing capacity to care for children. I have met families who have adopted profoundly disabled children, and who plainly love them very much. Families can get a lot of satisfaction if they feel they are making a difference to a child; whether the difference is weight gain, just a smile, the acquisition of some speech or even the slightest progress. Children with disabilities can thrive in families.

We already had three birth children when we adopted William. He was quite a bit younger than our other three and partly because of this, and partly because of his disability, there was less rivalry than there might have been. His disability brought out their compassionate side. Don't put potential families off. Ensure that they have realistic expectations about life with a child placed with them, but help them to retain their optimism and enthusiasm. Speaking with families who have already adopted can be enormously helpful.

Tip 6

Be a positive ambassador for disabled children

Disabled children can be inspiring. William has no self-pity, though he does question why he is disabled and sometimes, particularly now that he is older, he gets resentful about it. But on the whole, despite all he has to contend with, he is very positive and caring and works hard to get the most out of life. He has a friend who is blind and seeing the two of them together always cheers us up, with their positive outlook on life and their banter and humour. We think William's disability helped us to bond with him. He needed a lot of physical care and that brought us all close and may have helped to overcome the attachment difficulties he obviously had.

Families who adopt or foster disabled children often say that social workers paint gloomy pictures of children during the preparation and assessment process and later at the matching stage. It is important to strike a balance that retains the enthusiasm of potential carers but is also grounded in reality. The involvement of experienced adopters and foster carers in the preparation process makes the whole disability issue come alive.

Tip 7

Be generous with the support you offer families

Looking after disabled children can be hard work. At times it has felt like a battle to get the support we know William needs and the support we need as his parents. When William first came to us we had to battle to get transport to his nursery, which initially involved a one-hour drive there and back for my wife twice a day. We had to battle to get his educational needs met. (We heard it said at his mainstream secondary school that William was only expected to attend classes to keep him occupied. This confirmed our view that his education was not being taken seriously and, despite our initial wish that he should go to mainstream school, we then had to battle to get him enrolled in a special school, where he is doing well and has passed a number of certificated exams.) We receive small amount of respite care for William, but it is not enough and this is a source of ongoing strain – he needs our attention 24/7. It was important too that we continued to find time and space to give our other children the individual attention they needed. This would have been easier if we had received more support in looking after William.

Sometimes carers might want to adopt children they foster, including those with disabilities. Often this would be in the child's best interests. The carers and the child will have formed a relationship that can grow into something permanent. In Scotland the fostering regulations permit local authorities to continue paying the foster carers of children they adopt not only an adoption allowance but also the equivalent of a fostering fee for up to two years and in some circumstances longer. Foster carers may be reluctant to go down the adoption route out of concern that they will not continue to receive the same support from their local authority. Local authorities need to be willing to commit contractually to ensure that this is not a barrier to adoption for children who have this chance for permanency.

Tip 8

Regard the carers as equal members of the team around the child

William was underweight when he first came to us and was on various food supplements, which he plainly did not enjoy. My wife tried them herself and found them disgusting. She worked hard at finding what William liked to eat and to make it a more pleasurable experience. He began to like food, to put on weight and we threw the supplements away. He still needs encouragement to eat, but we have avoided the need for him to have a gastrostomy, which was a real possibility when he was younger. Carers are usually the best placed people to acquire knowledge and expertise, so listen to their views. It can be very hard for them if they are excluded from decision-making processes. We were not allowed to attend certain meetings where William's educational needs were discussed and this made us feel alienated and paranoid! But carers do not know everything and do get things wrong sometimes. They need to be open to new ideas and receptive to being challenged. It is important for professionals to establish an open relationship with families that is based on a balance of trust and challenge.

Tip 9

Be aware that social isolation is one of the most serious challenges facing children with disabilities

This has become more of a problem for William as he has grown older. When he was younger he was invited to the homes of classmates, but when he got larger wheelchairs and needed help with going to the toilet and so on, the invitations ceased. We still invited his friends to our house, but often they did not want to come because William is limited in the types of activity he can take part in. We are great supporters of inclusion, but increasingly William's friends come from the disabled world, and this often involves travelling fair distances to attend specialist sports clubs and social events. We recently took William on a 500-mile round trip to Sheffield to take part in a "Boccia" competition (a Paralympic ball sport introduced in 1984). Loneliness is an awful thing for children to have to deal with. Carers and those supporting them need to give disabled children the richest possible experience of both mainstream and specialist activities to help maximise their potential.

Tip10

Try and make the "disabled world" as easy for parents to find their way around as possible

There are about 20 or more professionals involved in William's life when you add up occupational therapists, physiotherapists, social workers, respite care staff, hospital consultants, and so on. Such a large cast of professionals can be overwhelming for new parents and also confusing; the distinction between who provides vital equipment like wheelchairs, walking frames, hoists and special beds is very complicated and varies depending on how services are organised locally. Let families choose their "key worker" or "lead professional" to work with them and help them to find their way around the system. Each child with complex needs would benefit from a tailor-made handbook to provide information about voluntary organisations that can offer valuable advice and support. Try to co-ordinate meetings, so that matters are dealt with holistically; make sure you and the family know what your role is. We have various appointments with people who simply seem to monitor William and we get nothing back from them. This can be very time consuming. Staff consistency is another problem. There is nothing worse than having to tell your story to one person only to find that they then leave and you have to start again with somebody else!

The bonus

In conclusion, being William's parents has been, and is, hard work, but he has enriched our lives and the lives of our children, our wider family and our friends. He has, we hope, had a happy childhood. He will be our son forever. At times he tells us he is going to leave home and go to college soon, like our other children have done. At times he gets cross with us and announces that he has had enough and never wanted to live with us anyway (He is a teenager!). At times he tells us he loves our house and to make sure we leave it to him in our will! At times he tells us he loves *us*. From our point of view adoption has been one of our better decisions in life and we would do it all over again.

Appendix

Ten of the more common disabilities and implications for care

There are a great many specific conditions and rare syndromes that impair functioning and may be termed a disability. A comprehensive directory is published by Contact a Family – see Resources section at the end of this book.

1. Autistic spectrum disorder

Autistic spectrum disorder (ASD) affects how the brain functions, usually causing difficulties with social interaction and communication. Asperger's syndrome is one of the disorders in the range of ASD. About two to three people in every 1000 have ASD, with males three times more likely to be affected. Symptoms usually appear at under, or around, two years old. They vary and range from mild to severe; some people have learning difficulties, while others excel academically, often in particular areas. The cause of ASD is unknown but there is ongoing research into hereditary and/or environmental factors. There is no cure and someone with ASD will always have difficulties, although their symptoms may change. Treatment tends to focus on the areas of support and therapeutic input. It is really important that you find out how this medical condition specifically impacts on this particular child, as this may vary widely.

2. Cerebral palsy

About one in every 500 children has cerebral palsy. It is the name given to a range of conditions which affect movement and are caused by damage to the brain while a baby is in the womb, or during or shortly after birth. Cerebral palsy affects different people in different ways, can vary from very mild to severe, and can affect all or part of the body. Children with cerebral palsy may have difficulty moving their muscles, or not enough control over their movements. There is no cure, but treatment often includes regular physiotherapy sessions to assist movement. Other types of support may include medication, speech therapy or occupational therapy.

3. Cystic fibrosis

Cystic fibrosis is a life-tehreatening inherited condition affecting over 7,500 people in the UK. It causes the lungs and other internal organs to become clogged with thick, sticky mucus. This makes it hard to breathe and digest food, which can lead to infections and poor weight gain. Cystic fibrosis affects one in every 2,500 babies. Treatment includes medication, a special diet to help weight gain, and physiotherapy to clear the mucus, which parents and carers can be taught. Although there is currently no cure, treatment has improved in recent years and many children will live well into adulthood.

4. Down's syndrome

Down's syndrome is the most common chromosomal disorder, affecting one person in every 1000, and it is one of the most common causes of learning difficulties. The severity with which a person will be affected varies, but there will usually be some health problems, developmental delay and distinctive facial features. Down's syndrome occurs across all ethnic groups and in both genders. With suitable treatment and support, average life expectancy is about 60 years.

5. Epilepsy

Epilepsy is common and can develop at any age. It is characterised by recurrent seizures, which occur when there is abnormal electrical activity in the brain. 'Generalised' seizures involve both sides of the brain and consciousness is lost; 'partial' seizures involve a specific part of the brain and consciousness is not lost, or impaired only slightly. About two-thirds of childhood seizures are partial. Epilepsy may result from a disability, an accident or illness involving brain trauma, a genetic predisposition or it may have no known cause. It is managed or treated with anti-convulsant medication. About a third of children 'grow out' of their epilepsy by the time they reach adulthood. Many will still need medication on a long-term basis.

6. Foetal alcohol spectrum disorders (FASD)

The term foetal alcohol spectrum disorders (FASD) is used to describe a wide range of disorders affecting children whose birth mother misused alcohol during pregnancy. They are also known as foetal alcohol syndrome (FAS) or foetal alcohol effects (FAE). It is not clear what level of alcohol use – including volume, frequency and duration – can trigger structural damage to the brain in unborn babies.

Characteristics of FAS often include abnormalities of growth, a weakened immune system and certain facial characteristics. Children with some, but not all, of these characteristics are said to have FAE. Most babies with FASD will seem irritable, have trouble eating and sleeping, and be sensitive to sensory stimulation. They may also have some level of developmental delay and learning difficulties at a later stage. FASD cannot be cured, but with consistency, support and loving care, children can be helped to understand and live with their condition.

7. Hydrocephalus

Hydrocephalus occurs when there is too much fluid in the brain because it does not drain away as it should. This fluid is called cerebrospinal fluid. To treat this condition, many people benefit from having a thin tube, or 'shunt', inserted into the brain. This drains the fluid to another part of the body, as normally happens with people who do not have hydrocephalus. As the shunt is usually permanent, it is important to have regular medical appointments to monitor progress and prevent infection.

The cause of hydrocephalus is not known, but it is thought to be due to damage to the brain or the blood supply to the brain, an infection, or another condition such as spina bifida. It may be present at birth (congenital) or may develop later. Babies with hydrocephalus may have an enlarged head and symptoms such as vomiting, poor feeding and irritability. Children with hydrocephalus may have developmental delay and behavioural and learning difficulties.

8. Microcephaly

Children have microcephaly when the circumference of their head is smaller than is age appropriate, either because the brain has not developed properly or it has stopped growing. It is more usual for the brain to be normally formed, despite its smaller size.

Microcephaly is often evident at birth and its cause can either be genetic or non-genetic. Where it is genetic, it is often a symptom of conditions such as Down's syndrome. Non-genetic reasons include maternal misuse of drugs or alcohol during pregnancy.

Children with microcephaly have various neurological impairments, from mild learning difficulties to cerebral palsy, but not all will have developmental delay. It really does depend on the child and any accompanying conditions they may have. Their development will be monitored throughout childhood and additional support – therapeutic or medicated – will be offered as needed.

9. Sickle cell anaemia/sickle cell disorders/sickle cell trait

Due to an abnormality of the haemoglobin in the bloodstream this condition can cause painful swellings of the hands and feet, infections, anaemia and pains in the joints and abdomen. Particularly painful episodes are known as "painful crises" and may have been brought on by strenuous exercise, dehydration, anaesthetics or infections – all of which have implications for care. A crisis can be mild, managed with over-the-counter painkillers, or extremely painful, needing hospital treatment. Other problems associated with sickle cell anaemia are jaundice, strokes, blood in the urine, leg ulcers and delayed growth. The condition is more common in people of African-Caribbean or Mediterranean origins.

Although there is no absolute cure for sickle cell anaemia, many people have had considerable success with bone marrow and stem cell transplants, particularly effective for young people aged under 16 years. However, the procedure has potentially serious side-effects. Other medical treatments, such as using umbilical cord blood, are in their early days but possibly hold great promise for the future.

10. Spina bifida

Spina bifida occurs when the newborn baby has part of its spinal cord and coverings exposed through a gap in the backbone. The resulting disabilities may include paralysis of the legs, incontinence and brain damage, but need not result in major impairment. The extent of the damage depends on the type of spina bifida and on the site of the defect.

A number of different treatments can be used to treat symptoms or conditions associated with spina bifida. They include: surgery on the spine or to treat hydrocephalus; therapies to help improve day-to-day life and boost independence; assistive technology, such as a manual or electric wheelchair or computer software to help with schoolwork and writing; and treatments for bowel and urinary problems.

Bibliography

References

Argent H (1998) "Who wants George?" Recruiting alternative families for children with disabilities, *Adoption & Fostering* 22:1, pp. 40–45

Argent H (ed) (2003) *Models of Adoption Support: What works and what doesn't?*, London: BAAF

Argent H (2006) *Ten Top Tips for Placing Children with Permanent Families*, London: BAAF

Argent H and Kerrane A (1997) *Taking Extra Care: Respite, shared and permanent care for children with disabilities*, London: BAAF

Baldwin S (1985) *The Cost of Caring*, London: Routledge & Kegan Paul

Bartram P and Clifford S and J (2013) *Parenting a Child with Developmental Delay*, London: BAAF

Cousins J (2005) 'Disabled children who need permanence: barriers to placement', *Adoption & Fostering* 29:3, pp. 6–20

Cousins J (2006) *Good Practice Guide: Every child is special*, London: BAAF

Hartley J (2012) 'Parenting the children of drug users', in Forrester D, *Parenting a Child Affected by Parental Substance Misuse*, London: BAAF

Macaskill C (2002) 'Managing contact arrangements for children with learning difficulties', in Argent H (ed), *Staying Connected*, London: BAAF.

Marsden R (2008) *The Family Business: The story of a family's adoption of a boy with cerebral palsy*, London: BAAF

Roberts J and H (2013) 'We adopted two autistic children', in Carter P, *Parenting a Child with Autistic Spectrum Disorder*, London: BAAF

Rowe J and Lambert L (1973) *Children Who Wait: A study of children needing substitute families*, London: BAAF

Sawbridge P (1975) *Opening New Doors*, London: BAAF

Sturge-Moore L (ed.) (2005) *Could you be my Parent? Adoption and fostering stories*, London: BAAF

Turnpenny P (2014) *Parenting a Child with, or at Risk of Genetic Disorders*, London: BAAF

Wedge P and Thoburn J (1986) *Placements by Parents for Children in Finding Families for "Hard to Place Children"*, London: BAAF

Recommended reading for adopters, foster carers, prospective carers and practitioners

Argent H (1998) *Whatever Happened to Adam? Stories of disabled people who were adopted or fostered*, London: BAAF
Tells the stories of 20 youngsters with disabilities and the families who chose to care for them. Using the words of the families themselves these stories are a testament to the commitment they offer to the disabled children.

Atwell A (2007) 'Working with children with a learning disability', in Ryan T and Walker R, *Life Story Work: A practical guide to helping children understand their past*, pp. 70–73, London: BAAF
'Children with a disability have the same "child" needs as any other child, and this means having an accurate account of their personal history.' So begins Ann Atwell's brief chapter on conducting life story work with children with a disability. The main focus is on communication – who is best able to understand the child and the methods most suitable to their needs.

Cairns K and Stanway C (2013) *Learn the Child: Helping looked after children to learn*, London: BAAF
Devised and written by a foster carer and social worker, and a Special Educational Needs teacher, this highly practical resource recommends ways in which looked after children can be best supported in their learning, and what teachers in the classroom, foster carers at home,

and social workers and other professionals working with children in different settings can do to help. Comprises a book, CD-Rom and case studies.

Cousins J (2011) *Ten Top Tips: Making matches*, London: BAAF
This book, aimed at practitioners and social work managers, takes the reader through some fundamental steps that workers can take to ensure that the matching process is as well thought through and carefully considered as possible – including 'Don't treat disabled children differently' (Tip 2).

Parenting Matters

This BAAF series, written by experts and parents, looks behind the diagnoses and "labels" that many looked after children bring with them.

Bartram P and Clifford S and J (2013) *Parenting a Child with Developmental Delay*, London: BAAF
Explores the topic of developmental delay, including assessment, symptoms and prognosis and what this means for children. Highlights the importance of focusing not only on the condition but also on the child as a whole person, including their personality, emotional well-being and life experiences.

Carter P (2013) *Parenting a Child with Autism Spectrum Disorder*, London: BAAF
Explains autism and how it affects communication, social interaction and restricted or repetitive interests of a child with this condition; explores symptoms, prognosis and treatment, including appropriate medication, training and coaching.

Forrester D (2012) *Parenting a Child Affected by Parental Substance Abuse*, London: BAAF
Investigates the issues surrounding substance misuse and children entering care as well as the impact on children of exposure to substances during pregnancy. Includes specific conditions like Foetal Alcohol Syndrome, and wider issues, such as genetic susceptibilities.

Hughes D (2013) *Parenting a Child with Emotional and Behavioural Difficulties*, London: BAAF
Hughes looks at emotional and behavioural difficulties commonly experienced in looked after children. He shares his considerable

expertise on the symptoms, prognosis and treatment of affected children, and provides advice on how parents and carers can help children to improve their behaviour and increase their self-esteem.

Jackson C (2012) *Parenting a Child with Mental Health Issues*, London: BAAF
Provides a general explanation of mental disorders and how they may manifest in children and outlines the risk for a child with a family history of mental health problems and the genetic and environmental factors that increase the risk. Physiological processes that may explain a child's behaviours and their vulnerability to mental disorder are also examined.

Jacobs B and Miles L (2012) *Parenting a Child with Attention Deficit Hyperactivity Disorder*, London: BAAF
Explains ADHD and related conditions in children and young people, including symptoms, prognosis and treatment, and looks at the ways in which this condition can affect child development and behaviour, the issues about educational provision for affected children and where and how to get help.

Turnpenny PD (2014) *Parenting a Child with, or at Risk of, Genetic Disorders*, London: BAAF
Examines the effects of genetics on human health and explains how genetic disorders may pass through families. Turnpenny goes on to explore what parents can do when a child, or a child's birth parents, have or may have a genetic disease, and looks at the issues regarding genetic testing of adopted children.

Journal articles

Cousins J (2009) 'Disability: still taboo in family placement?', *Adoption & Fostering* 33:2, pp. 54–65
The starting point for this exploration into the place of disabled children in the context of adoption and foster care is the observation that when children in need are portrayed, the picture is one of a generic, not-disabled child; that disabled children have an untouchable status which profoundly affects their life chances; that they are at the margins of our consciousness; and that, in some measure, disability is still taboo in family placement. The principal argument is that disabled

children are not a separate group, but are the responsibility of everyone engaged in working on behalf of young people. The taboo must be lifted.

Cousins J and Simmonds J (2011) 'Investigating the involvement of disabled children in using In My Shoes as a family-finding tool: a pilot project', *Adoption & Fostering* 35:4, pp. 4–19
Engaging meaningfully with children in the family-finding process presents an additional challenge to social workers when the child is disabled. This project explored the use of an interactive computer interview, *In My Shoes*, with disabled children for whom a permanent new family was being sought. *In My Shoes* uses accessible and child-friendly images to aid communication between worker and child. It is suitable for children aged three years and over, and has been demonstrated to engage children who have a wide range of abilities.

Resources for children

Illustrated guides

Argent H (2004) *What is a Disability? A guide for children and young people*, London: BAAF
Explains what disabilities are and what it can mean for children who might have them. It tells the stories of some children who are disabled and explains what they can and can't do. Simple questions encourage the child to think about what having a disability may mean.

Shah S (2003) *Fostering: What it is and what it means – a guide for children and young people*, London: BAAF
Describes in accessible and jargon-free language: what fostering is; how it differs from adoption; different types of fostering; how children come to be fostered; what foster carers do; identifying and then moving in with the right foster family; care plans; birth parents and contact; school and health matters.

Shah S (2012) *Adoption: What it is and what it means – a guide for children and young people*, London: BAAF
Covers crucial questions on the adoption process and procedure such as: What is adoption? How is adoption different from fostering? How is adoption decided on? How will the right family be found? What happens in court?

Shah S and Argent H (2006) *Life Story Work: What it is and what it means – a guide for children and young people*, London: BAAF
Explores the importance of life stories, including those of several famous people ,and parallels these with the child's own story. Describes the process of undertaking life story work, who can help and how, when to do it, what goes in it and who owns the work. Also demonstrates imaginative techniques and different media that can be used.

Illustrated stories

Yarney S (2014) *My Brother Boo has ADHD*, London: BAAF
This story about a boy with ADHD will be helpful for any child aged 7 to 11 who finds it difficult to stay still or pay attention, or whose behaviour often gets them into trouble. It will also be useful for a child who knows someone with the condition. Includes a question and answer section covering a range of queries and concerns about ADHD.

Miles L (2014) *Sam's Trouble with Words: A story about a boy with dyslexia*, London: BAAF
Recommended for any child aged 7 to 11 who has difficulty reading and writing, or who knows someone who does. Includes a question-and-answer section featuring queries and concerns about dyslexia.

Jackson C (2014) *Oli and the Pink Bicycle: A story about a girl born with Foetal Alcohol Syndrome*, London: BAAF
Helpful for any child aged 7 to 11 whose development and behaviour has been affected by parental substance misuse, or who knows someone who is affected. Again, includes a question and answer section covering a range of queries and concerns about FAS.

Inter-active materials for work with children

Ahmad A and Betts B (2003) *My Life Story* (CD/ROM) Information Plus, available from BAAF
This interactive CD-ROM aims to lead the child and adult through a range of life story activities to help them come to terms with the loss of their birth family, to understand the reasons why they are looked after and to think positively about the future. It also provides opportunities for individual support and counselling.

Argent H (2012) *Moving Pictures*, London: BAAF
An essential tool to help children explore ideas of moving and permanence. It consists of a CD ROM with printable black-and-white illustrations of aspects of moving to permanence (which the child can colour), designed to spark discussion about a child's wishes and hopes in preparation for moving to a new family.

Camis J (2001) *My Life and Me*, London: BAAF
This durable and comprehensive workbook provides much-needed help to children separated from their family of origin, enabling them to record accurate knowledge of their past and their family. Once completed, the book provides a permanent record which they, and the adults caring for them, can refer to at any time. Can be used flexibly by any child, including children with special needs.

Maye J (2011) *Me and my Family: A book for adopted children and their families to get to know each other*, London: BAAF
A colourful, easy-to-use resource enabling children and their new families to capture and share their experiences of adoption, work through any issues or concerns, and plan a stable and loving future.

Useful organisations

The Advisory Centre for Education (ACE):
www.ace-ed.org.uk
Helpline: 0808 800 5793
Provides independent advice for parents and carers of children aged 5–16 in state-funded education. Also see IPSEA below.

Capability Scotland:
www.capability-scotland.org.uk
Campaigns with and provides education, employment and care services for disabled children and adults across Scotland.

Contact a Family:
www.cafamily.org.uk
Tel: 020 7608 8700; Helpline: 0808 808 3555
Provides support, advice and information for families with disabled children, no matter what their situation or disability.

Down's Syndrome Association:
www.downs-syndrome.org.uk
Helps support people with Down's syndrome and their families throughout their lives. Welcomes adopters, carers and professionals.

Independent Parental Special Needs Advice (IPSEA):
www.ipsea.org.uk
Helpline: 0800 018 4016
Offers free and independent legally-based information, advice and support to help get the right education for children and young people with all kinds of special educational needs and disabilities (SEND).

KIDS:
Kids.org.uk
Works with disabled children, young people and their families across England offering a range of services for those with disabilities and developmental problems.

Mencap:
mencap.org.uk
Tel (England): 020 7454 0454; (Northern Ireland) 020 7454 0454 ; (Wales/Cymru) 02920 747 588
Supports people with learning disabilities and their families and carers.

National Autistic Society:
www.autism.org.uk
Tel: 0808 800 4104
Provides information, support and services aimed at supporting anyone with autism.

Netbuddy:
www.netbuddy.org.uk
Recently merged with Scope below, Netbuddy provides a place for the parents of disbled children to share experiences, swap practical tips and exchange information online.

Scope (England and Wales):
scope.org.uk
Tel: 0808 800 3333
Supports people with cerebral palsy and their families and carers.